The White Wampum

E. Pauline Johnson

The White Wampum
by E. Pauline Johnson

First collection of poetry, published in London in 1895

CONTENTS

The White Wampum

Ojistoh

I am Ojistoh, I am she, the wife
Of him whose name breathes bravery and life
And courage to the tribe that calls him chief.
I am Ojistoh, his white star, and he
Is land, and lake, and sky—and soul to me.

Ah! but they hated him, those Huron braves,
Him who had flung their warriors into graves,
Him who had crushed them underneath his heel,
Whose arm was iron, and whose heart was steel
To all—save me, Ojistoh, chosen wife
Of my great Mohawk, white star of his life.

Ah! but they hated him, and councilled long
With subtle witchcraft how to work him wrong;
How to avenge their dead, and strike him where
His pride was highest, and his fame most fair.
Their hearts grew weak as women at his name:
They dared no war-path since my Mohawk came
With ashen bow, and flinten arrow-head
To pierce their craven bodies; but their dead
Must be avenged. Avenged? They dared not walk
In day and meet his deadly tomahawk;
They dared not face his fearless scalping knife;
So—Niyoh![1]—then they thought of me, his wife.

O! evil, evil face of them they sent
With evil Huron speech: "Would I consent
To take of wealth? be queen of all their tribe?
Have wampum ermine?" Back I flung the bribe
Into their teeth, and said, "While I have life
Know this—Ojistoh is the Mohawk's wife."

Wah! how we struggled! But their arms were strong.
They flung me on their pony's back, with thong
Round ankle, wrist, and shoulder. Then upleapt
The one I hated most: his eye he swept
Over my misery, and sneering said,
"Thus, fair Ojistoh, we avenge our dead."

1

Handwritten annotations:

- confidence, identity
- unity
- nature united
- Native tribal National
- No name?
- guiding star
- soulmates
- God like. superhuman quality.
- physical power / strength.
- only emotional exception.
- terrified of him, dare not take revenge on their dead.
- weapons.
- Native name for God.
- his wife is his weakness. the only way to avenge.
- They are evil.
- try to bribe her to be part of their tribe.
- seperates her husband from this evil tribe.

The White Wampum

And we two rode, rode as a sea wind-chased,
I, bound with buckskin to his hated waist,
He, sneering, laughing, jeering, while he lashed
The horse to foam, as on and on we dashed.
Plunging through creek and river, bush and trail,
On, on we galloped like a northern gale.
At last, his distant Huron fires aflame
We saw, and nearer, nearer still we came.

listing, emphasises these negative aspects. progression of a dangerous journey.

I, bound behind him in the captive's place,
Scarcely could see the outline of his face.
I smiled, and laid my cheek against his back:
"Loose thou my hands," I said. "This pace let slack.
Forget we now that thou and I are foes.
I like thee well, and wish to clasp thee close;
I like the courage of thine eye and brow;
I like thee better than my Mohawk now."

Tries to seduce him to set her free.

He cut the cords; we ceased our maddened haste
I wound my arms about his tawny waist;
My hand crept up the buckskin of his belt;
His knife hilt in my burning palm I felt;
One hand caressed his cheek, the other drew
The weapon softly—"I love you, love you,"
I whispered, "love you as my life."
And—buried in his back his scalping knife.

Uses her clever female qualities.

—not emphasised

Ha! how I rode, rode as a sea wind-chased,
Mad with sudden freedom, mad with haste,
Back to my Mohawk and my home. I lashed
That horse to foam, as on and on I dashed.
Plunging thro' creek and river, bush and trail,
On, on I galloped like a northern gale.
And then my distant Mohawk's fires aflame
I saw, as nearer, nearer still I came,
My hands all wet, stained with a life's red dye,
But pure my soul, pure as those stars on high—
"My Mohawk's pure white star, Ojistoh, still am I."

even though she killed she's still pure.

she comes back the way she was, still Mohawks wife.

Footnotes

1   God, in the Mohawk language.

2

The White Wampum

As Red Men Die

third person.

Captive! Is there a hell to him like this?
A taunt more galling than the Huron's hiss?
He—proud and scornful, he—who laughed at law,
He—scion of the deadly Iroquois,
He—the bloodthirsty, he—the Mohawk chief,
He—who despises pain and sneers at grief,
Here in the hated Huron's vicious clutch,
That even captive he disdains to touch!

sense of shame

Not praising him as she did before.

Captive! But *never* conquered; Mohawk brave
Stoops not to be to *any* man a slave;
Least, to the puny tribe his soul abhors,
The tribe whose wigwams sprinkle Simcoe's shores.
With scowling brow he stands and courage high,
Watching with haughty and defiant eye
His captors, as they council o'er his fate,
Or strive his boldness to intimidate.
Then fling they unto him the choice;

he is still very much in control.

        "Wilt thou
Walk o'er the bed of fire that waits thee now—
Walk with uncovered feet upon the coals,
Until thou reach the ghostly Land of Souls,
And, with thy Mohawk death-song please our ear?
Or wilt thou with the women rest thee here?"
His eyes flash like an eagle's, and his hands
Clench at the insult. Like a god he stands.
"Prepare the fire!" he scornfully demands.

testing his manliness.

He knoweth not that this same jeering band
Will bite the dust—will lick the Mohawk's hand;
Will kneel and cower at the Mohawk's feet;
Will shrink when Mohawk war drums wildly beat.

His death will be avenged with hideous hate
By Iroquois, swift to annihilate
His vile detested captors, that now flaunt
Their war clubs in his face with sneer and taunt,
Not thinking, soon that reeking, red, and raw,
Their scalps will deck the belts of Iroquois.

The White Wampum

The path of coals outstretches, white with heat,
A forest fir's length—ready for his feet.
Unflinching as a rock he steps along
The burning mass, and sings his wild war song;
Sings, as he sang when once he used to roam
Throughout the forests of his southern home,
Where, down the Genesee, the water roars,
Where gentle Mohawk purls between its shores,
Songs, that of exploit and of prowess tell;
Songs of the Iroquois invincible.

Up the long trail of fire he boasting goes,
Dancing a war dance to defy his foes.
His flesh is scorched, his muscles burn and shrink,
But still he dances to death's awful brink.

The eagle plume that crests his haughty head
Will *never* droop until his heart be dead.
Slower and slower yet his footstep swings,
Wilder and wilder still his death-song rings,
Fiercer and fiercer thro' the forest bounds
His voice that leaps to Happier Hunting Grounds.
One savage yell—

       Then loyal to his race,
He bends to death—but *never* to disgrace.

He will be the strong man
everyone knows
until the end.
Keeps his reputation
and dignity
until he dies.

The Pilot of the Plains

"False," they said, "thy Pale-face lover, from the land of waking morn;
Rise and wed thy Redskin wooer, nobler warrior ne'er was born;
Cease thy watching, cease thy dreaming,
　　Show the white thine Indian scorn."

Thus they taunted her, declaring, "He remembers naught of thee:
Likely some white maid he wooeth, far beyond the inland sea."
But she answered ever kindly,
　　"He will come again to me,"

Till the dusk of Indian summer crept athwart the western skies;
But a deeper dusk was burning in her dark and dreaming eyes,
As she scanned the rolling prairie,
　　Where the foothills fall, and rise.

Till the autumn came and vanished, till the season of the rains,
Till the western world lay fettered in midwinter's crystal chains,
Still she listened for his coming,
　　Still she watched the distant plains.

Then a night with nor'land tempest, nor'land snows a-swirling fast,
Out upon the pathless prairie came the Pale-face through the blast,
Calling, calling, "Yakonwita,
　　I am coming, love, at last."

Hovered night above, about him, dark its wings and cold and dread;
Never unto trail or tepee were his straying footsteps led;
Till benumbed, he sank, and pillowed
　　On the drifting snows his head,

Saying, "O! my Yakonwita call me, call me, be my guide
To the lodge beyond the prairie—for I vowed ere winter died
I would come again, beloved;
　　I would claim my Indian bride."

"Yakonwita, Yakonwita!" Oh, the dreariness that strains
Through the voice that calling, quivers, till a whisper but remains,
"Yakonwita, Yakonwita,
　　I am lost upon the plains."

But the Silent Spirit hushed him, lulled him as he cried anew,
"Save me, save me! O! beloved, I am Pale but I am true.
Yakonwita, Yakonwita,
   I am dying, love, for you."

Leagues afar, across the prairie, she had risen from her bed,
Roused her kinsmen from their slumber: "He has come to-night," she said.
"I can hear him calling, calling;
   But his voice is as the dead.

"Listen!" and they sate all silent, while the tempest louder grew,
And a spirit-voice called faintly, "I am dying, love, for you."
Then they wailed, "O! Yakonwita.
   He was Pale, but he was true."

Wrapped she then her ermine round her, stepped without the tepee door,
Saying, "I must follow, follow, though he call for evermore,
Yakonwita, Yakonwita;"
   And they never saw her more.

Late at night, say Indian hunters, when the starlight clouds or wanes,
Far away they see a maiden, misty as the autumn rains,
Guiding with her lamp of moonlight
   Hunters lost upon the plains.

The Cattle Thief

They were coming across the prairie, they were
    galloping hard and fast;
For the eyes of those desperate riders had sighted
    their man at last—
Sighted him off to Eastward, where the Cree
    encampment lay,
Where the cotton woods fringed the river, miles and
    miles away.
Mistake him? Never! Mistake him? the famous
    Eagle Chief!
That terror to all the settlers, that desperate Cattle
    Thief—
That monstrous, fearless Indian, who lorded it over
    the plain,
Who thieved and raided, and scouted, who rode like
    a hurricane!
But they've tracked him across the prairie; they've
    followed him hard and fast;
For those desperate English settlers have sighted
    their man at last.

Up they wheeled to the tepees, all their British
    blood aflame,
Bent on bullets and bloodshed, bent on bringing
    down their game;
But they searched in vain for the Cattle Thief: that
    lion had left his lair,
And they cursed like a troop of demons—for the
    women alone were there.
"The sneaking Indian coward," they hissed; "he
    hides while yet he can;
He'll come in the night for cattle, but he's scared
    to face a *man*."
"Never!" and up from the cotton woods rang the
    voice of Eagle Chief;
And right out into the open stepped, unarmed, the
    Cattle Thief.
Was that the game they had coveted? Scarce fifty
    years had rolled

Over that fleshless, hungry frame, starved to the
    bone and old;
Over that wrinkled, tawny skin, unfed by the
    warmth of blood.
Over those hungry, hollow eyes that glared for the
    sight of food.

He turned, like a hunted lion: "I know not fear,"
    said he;
And the words outleapt from his shrunken lips in
    the language of the Cree.
"I'll fight you, white-skins, one by one, till I
    kill you *all*," he said;
But the threat was scarcely uttered, ere a dozen
    balls of lead
Whizzed through the air about him like a shower
    of metal rain,
And the gaunt old Indian Cattle Thief dropped
    dead on the open plain.
And that band of cursing settlers gave one
    triumphant yell,
And rushed like a pack of demons on the body that
    writhed and fell.
"Cut the fiend up into inches, throw his carcass
    on the plain;
Let the wolves eat the cursed Indian, he'd have
    treated us the same."
A dozen hands responded, a dozen knives gleamed
    high,
But the first stroke was arrested by a woman's
    strange, wild cry.
And out into the open, with a courage past
    belief,
She dashed, and spread her blanket o'er the corpse
    of the Cattle Thief;
And the words outleapt from her shrunken lips in
    the language of the Cree,
"If you mean to touch that body, you must cut
    your way through *me*."
And that band of cursing settlers dropped
    backward one by one,
For they knew that an Indian woman roused, was
    a woman to let alone.

And then she raved in a frenzy that they scarcely
  understood,
Raved of the wrongs she had suffered since her
  earliest babyhood:
"Stand back, stand back, you white-skins, touch
  that dead man to your shame;
You have stolen my father's spirit, but his body I
  only claim.
You have killed him, but you shall not dare to
  touch him now he's dead.
You have cursed, and called him a Cattle Thief,
  though you robbed him first of bread—
Robbed him and robbed my people—look there, at
  that shrunken face,
Starved with a hollow hunger, we owe to you and
  your race.
What have you left to us of land, what have you
  left of game,
What have you brought but evil, and curses since
  you came?
How have you paid us for our game? how paid us
  for our land?
By a *book*, to save our souls from the sins *you*
  brought in your other hand.
Go back with your new religion, we never have
  understood
Your robbing an Indian's *body*, and mocking his
  soul with food.
Go back with your new religion, and find—if find
  you can—
The *honest* man you have ever made from out a
  starving man.
You say your cattle are not ours, your meat is not
  our meat;
When *you* pay for the land you live in, *we'll* pay
  for the meat we eat.
Give back our land and our country, give back our
  herds of game;
Give back the furs and the forests that were ours
  before you came;

9

Give back the peace and the plenty. Then come
   with your new belief,
And blame, if you dare, the hunger that *drove* him to
   be a thief."

The White Wampum

A Cry from an Indian Wife

[handwritten: — contrast to europeans.]

My forest brave, my Red-skin love, farewell;
We may not meet to-morrow; who can tell
What mighty ills befall our little band,
Or what you'll suffer from the white man's hand?
Here is your knife! I thought 'twas sheathed for aye.
No roaming bison calls for it to-day;
No hide of prairie cattle will it maim;
The plains are bare, it seeks a nobler game:
'Twill drink the life-blood of a soldier host.
Go; rise and strike, no matter what the cost.
Yet stay. Revolt not at the Union Jack,
Nor raise Thy hand against this stripling pack
Of white-faced warriors, marching West to quell
Our fallen tribe that rises to rebel.
They all are young and beautiful and good;
Curse to the war that drinks their harmless blood.
Curse to the fate that brought them from the East
To be our chiefs—to make our nation least
That breathes the air of this vast continent.
Still their new rule and council is well meant.
They but forget we Indians owned the land
From ocean unto ocean; that they stand
Upon a soil that centuries agone
Was our sole kingdom and our right alone.
They never think how they would feel to-day,
If some great nation came from far away,
Wresting their country from their hapless braves,
Giving what they gave us—but wars and graves.
Then go and strike for liberty and life,
And bring back honour to your Indian wife.
Your wife? Ah, what of that, who cares for me?
Who pities my poor love and agony?
What white-robed priest prays for your safety here,
As prayer is said for every volunteer
That swells the ranks that Canada sends out?
Who prays for vict'ry for the Indian scout?
Who prays for our poor nation lying low?
None—therefore take your tomahawk and go.
My heart may break and burn into its core,
But I am strong to bid you go to war.

[handwritten: unable to make up her mind, be aggressive or passive.]

11

Yet stay, my heart is not the only one
That grieves the loss of husband and of son;
Think of the mothers o'er the inland seas;
Think of the pale-faced maiden on her knees;
One pleads her God to guard some sweet-faced child
That marches on toward the North-West wild.
The other prays to shield her love from harm,
To strengthen his young, proud uplifted arm.
Ah, how her white face quivers thus to think,
Your tomahawk his life's best blood will drink.
She never thinks of my wild aching breast,
Nor prays for your dark face and eagle crest
Endangered by a thousand rifle balls,
My heart the target if my warrior falls.
O! coward self I hesitate no more;
Go forth, and win the glories of the war.
Go forth, nor bend to greed of white men's hands,
By right, by birth we Indians own these lands,
Though starved, crushed, plundered, lies our nation low…
Perhaps the white man's God has willed it so.

Finally says go to war
this is our land!

Dawendine

There's a spirit on the river, there's a ghost upon the shore,
They are chanting, they are singing through the starlight evermore,
As they steal amid the silence,
   And the shadows of the shore.

You can hear them when the Northern candles light the Northern sky,
Those pale, uncertain candle flames, that shiver, dart and die,
Those dead men's icy finger tips,
   Athwart the Northern sky.

You can hear the ringing war-cry of a long-forgotten brave
Echo through the midnight forest, echo o'er the midnight wave,
And the Northern lanterns tremble
   At the war-cry of that brave.

And you hear a voice responding, but in soft and tender song;
It is Dawendine's spirit singing, singing all night long;
And the whisper of the night wind
   Bears afar her Spirit song.

And the wailing pine trees murmur with their voice attuned to hers,
Murmur when they 'rouse from slumber as the night wind through
them stirs;
And you listen to their legend,
   And their voices blend with hers.

There was feud and there was bloodshed near the river by the hill;
And Dawendine listened, while her very heart stood still:
Would her kinsman or her lover
   Be the victim by the hill?

Who would be the great unconquered? who come boasting how he dealt
Death? and show his rival's scalplock fresh and bleeding at his belt.
Who would say, "O Dawendine!
   Look upon the death I dealt?"

And she listens, listens, listens—till a war-cry rends the night,
Cry of her victorious lover, monarch he of all the height;
And his triumph wakes the horrors,
   Kills the silence of the night.

The White Wampum

Heart of her! it throbs so madly, then lies freezing in her breast,
For the icy hand of death has chilled the brother she loved best;
And her lover dealt the death-blow;
    And her heart dies in her breast.

And she hears her mother saying, "Take thy belt of wampum white;
Go unto yon evil savage while he glories on the height;
Sing and sue for peace between us:
    At his feet lay wampum white.

"Lest thy kinsmen all may perish, all thy brothers and thy sire
Fall before his mighty hatred as the forest falls to fire;
Take thy wampum pale and peaceful,
    Save thy brothers, save thy sire."

And the girl arises softly, softly slips toward the shore;
Loves she well the murdered brother, loves his hated foeman more,
Loves, and longs to give the wampum;
    And she meets him on the shore.

"Peace," she sings, "O mighty victor, Peace! I bring thee wampum white.
Sheathe thy knife whose blade has tasted my young kinsman's blood to-night
Ere it drink to slake its thirsting,
    I have brought thee wampum white."

Answers he, "O Dawendine! I will let thy kinsmen be,
I accept thy belt of wampum; but my hate demands for me
That they give their fairest treasure,
    Ere I let thy kinsmen be.

"Dawendine, for thy singing, for thy suing, war shall cease;
For thy name, which speaks of dawning, *Thou* shalt be the dawn of peace;
For thine eyes whose purple shadows tell of dawn,
    My hate shall cease.

"Dawendine, Child of Dawning, hateful are thy kin to me;
Red my fingers with their heart blood, but my heart is red for thee:
Dawendine, Child of Dawning,
    Wilt thou fail or follow me?"

And her kinsmen still are waiting her returning from the night,
Waiting, waiting for her coming with her belt of wampum white;
But forgetting all, she follows,
  Where he leads through day or night.

There's a spirit on the river, there's a ghost upon the shore,
And they sing of love and loving through the starlight evermore,
As they steal amid the silence,
  And the shadows of the shore.

Wolverine

Speech structure builds a story

"Yes, sir, it's quite a story, though you won't believe it's true,
But such things happened often when I lived beyond the Soo."
And the trapper tilted back his chair and filled his pipe anew.

in dialect, shines through.

"I ain't thought of it neither fer this many 'n many a day,
Although it used to haunt me in the years that's slid away,
The years I spent a-trappin' for the good old Hudson's Bay.

"Wild? You bet, 'twas wild then, an' few an' far between
The squatters' shacks, for whites was scarce as furs when things is green,
An' only reds an' 'Hudson's' men was all the folk I seen.

not harmful.

"No. Them old Indyans ain't so bad, not if you treat 'em square.
Why, I lived in amongst 'em all the winters I was there,
An' I never lost a copper, an' I never lost a hair.

if you treat them well you'll do the same

"But I'd have lost my life the time that you've heard tell about;
I don't think I'd be settin' here, but dead beyond a doubt,
If that there Indyan 'Wolverine' jest hadn't helped me out.

"'Twas freshet time, 'way back, as long as sixty-six or eight,
An' I was comin' to the Post that year a kind of late,
For beaver had been plentiful, and trappin' had been great.

"One day I had been settin' traps along a bit of wood,
An' night was catchin' up to me jest faster 'an it should,
When all at once I heard a sound that curdled up my blood.

"It was the howl of famished wolves—I didn't stop to think
But jest lit out across for home as quick as you could wink,
But when I reached the river's edge I brought up at the brink.

"That mornin' I had crossed the stream straight on a sheet of ice
An' now, God help me! There it was, churned up an' cracked to dice,
The flood went boiling past—I stood like one shut in a vice.

"No way ahead, no path aback, trapped like a rat ashore,
With naught but death to follow, and with naught but death afore;
The howl of hungry wolves aback—ahead, the torrent's roar.

16

The White Wampum

"An' then—a voice, an Indyan voice, that called out clear and clean,
'Take Indyan's horse, I run like deer, wolf can't catch Wolverine.'
I says, 'Thank Heaven.' There stood the chief I'd nicknamed Wolverine.

"I leapt on that there horse, an' then jest like a coward fled,
An' left that Indyan standin' there alone, as good as dead,
With the wolves a-howlin' at his back, the swollen stream ahead.

"I don't know how them Indyans dodge from death the way they do,
You won't believe it, sir, but what I'm tellin' you is true,
But that there chap was 'round next day as sound as me or you.

"He came to get his horse, but not a cent he'd take from me.
Yes, sir, you're right, the Indyans now ain't like they used to be;
We've got 'em sharpened up a bit an' *now* they'll take a fee.

"No, sir, you're wrong, they ain't no 'dogs.' I'm not through tellin' yet;
You'll take that name right back again, or else jest out you get!
You'll take that name right back when you hear all this yarn, I bet.

"It happened that same autumn, when some Whites was comin' in,
I heard the old Red River carts a-kickin' up a din,
So I went over to their camp to see an English skin.

"They said, 'They'd had an awful scare from Injuns,' an' they swore
That savages had come around the very night before
A-brandishing their tomahawks an' painted up for war.

"But when their plucky Englishmen had put a bit of lead
Right through the heart of one of them, an' rolled him over, dead,
The other cowards said that they had come on peace instead.

Seen as a lower life .

"'That they (the Whites) had lost some stores, from off their little pack,
An' that the Red they peppered dead had followed up their track,
Because he'd found the packages an' came *to give them back.*'

"'Oh!' they said, 'they were quite sorry, but it wasn't like as if
They had killed a decent Whiteman by mistake or in a tiff,
It was only some old Injun dog that lay there stark an' stiff.'

"I said, 'You are the meanest dogs that ever yet I seen,'
Then I rolled the body over as it lay out on the green;
I peered into the face—My God! 'twas poor old Wolverine."

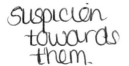
suspicion towards them.

Positive representation .

The Vagabonds

What saw you in your flight to-day,
Crows, awinging your homeward way?

Went you far in carrion quest,
Crows, that worry the sunless west?

Thieves and villains, you shameless things!
Black your record as black your wings.

Tell me, birds of the inky hue,
Plunderous rogues—to-day have you

Seen with mischievous, prying eyes
Lands where earlier suns arise?

Saw you a lazy beck between
Trees that shadow its breast in green,

Teased by obstinate stones that lie
Crossing the current tauntingly?

Fields abloom on the farther side
With purpling clover lying wide—

Saw you there as you circled by,
Vale-environed a cottage lie,

Girt about with emerald bands,
Nestling down in its meadow lands?

Saw you this on your thieving raids?
Speak—you rascally renegades!

Thieved you also away from me
Olden scenes that I long to see?

If, O! crows, you have flown since morn
Over the place where I was born,

The White Wampum

Forget will I, how black you were
Since dawn, in feather and character;

Absolve will I, your vagrant band
Ere you enter your slumberland.

The Song my Paddle Sings

West wind, blow from your prairie nest,
Blow from the mountains, blow from the west.
The sail is idle, the sailor too;
O! wind of the west, we wait for you.
Blow, blow!
I have wooed you so,
But never a favour you bestow.
You rock your cradle the hills between,
But scorn to notice my white lateen.

I stow the sail, unship the mast:
I wooed you long but my wooing's past;
My paddle will lull you into rest.
O! drowsy wind of the drowsy west,
Sleep, sleep,
By your mountain steep,
Or down where the prairie grasses sweep!
Now fold in slumber your laggard wings,
For soft is the song my paddle sings.

August is laughing across the sky,
Laughing while paddle, canoe and I,
Drift, drift,
Where the hills uplift
On either side of the current swift.

The river rolls in its rocky bed;
My paddle is plying its way ahead;
Dip, dip,
While the waters flip
In foam as over their breast we slip.

And oh, the river runs swifter now;
The eddies circle about my bow.
Swirl, swirl!
How the ripples curl
In many a dangerous pool awhirl!

And forward far the rapids roar,
Fretting their margin for evermore.

The White Wampum

Dash, dash,
With a mighty crash,
They seethe, and boil, and bound, and splash.

Be strong, O paddle! be brave, canoe!
The reckless waves you must plunge into.
Reel, reel.
On your trembling keel,
But never a fear my craft will feel.

We've raced the rapid, we're far ahead!
The river slips through its silent bed.
Sway, sway,
As the bubbles spray
And fall in tinkling tunes away.

And up on the hills against the sky,
A fir tree rocking its lullaby,
Swings, swings,
Its emerald wings,
Swelling the song that my paddle sings.

The Camper

Night 'neath the northern skies, lone, black, and grim:
Naught but the starlight lies 'twixt heaven, and him.

Of man no need has he, of God, no prayer;
He and his Deity are brothers there.

Above his bivouac the firs fling down
Through branches gaunt and black, their needles brown.

Afar some mountain streams, rockbound and fleet,
Sing themselves through his dreams in cadence sweet,

The pine trees whispering, the heron's cry,
The plover's passing wing, his lullaby.

And blinking overhead the white stars keep
Watch o'er his hemlock bed—his sinless sleep.

At Husking Time

At husking time the tassel fades
To brown above the yellow blades,
  Whose rustling sheath enswathes the corn
  That bursts its chrysalis in scorn
Longer to lie in prison shades.

Among the merry lads and maids
The creaking ox-cart slowly wades
Twixt stalks and stubble, sacked and torn
At husking time.

The prying pilot crow persuades
The flock to join in thieving raids;
The sly racoon with craft inborn
His portion steals; from plenty's horn
His pouch the saucy chipmunk lades
At husking time.

Workworn

Across the street, an humble woman lives;
To her 'tis little fortune ever gives;
Denied the wines of life, it puzzles me
To know how she can laugh so cheerily.
This morn I listened to her softly sing,
And, marvelling what this effect could bring
I looked: 'twas but the presence of a child
Who passed her gate, and looking in, had smiled.
But self-encrusted, I had failed to see
The child had also looked and laughed to me.
My lowly neighbour thought the smile God-sent,
And singing, through the toilsome hours she went.
O! weary singer, I have learned the wrong
Of taking gifts, and giving naught of song;
I thought my blessings scant, my mercies few,
Till I contrasted them with yours, and you;
To-day I counted much, yet wished it more—
While but a child's bright smile was all your store,

If I had thought of all the stormy days,
That fill some lives that tread less favoured ways,
How little sunshine through their shadows gleamed,
My own dull life had much the brighter seemed;
If I had thought of all the eyes that weep
Through desolation, and still smiling keep,
That see so little pleasure, so much woe,
My own had laughed more often long ago;
If I had thought how leaden was the weight
Adversity lays at my kinsman's gate,
Of that great cross my next door neighbour bears,
My thanks had been more frequent in my prayers;
If I had watched the woman o'er the way,
Workworn and old, who labours day by day,
Who has no rest, no joy to call her own,
My tasks, my heart, had much the lighter grown.

Easter

April 1, 1888

Lent gathers up her cloak of sombre shading
  In her reluctant hands.
Her beauty heightens, fairest in its fading,
  As pensively she stands
Awaiting Easter's benediction falling,
  Like silver stars at night,
Before she can obey the summons calling
  Her to her upward flight,
Awaiting Easter's wings that she must borrow
  Ere she can hope to fly —
Those glorious wings that we shall see to-morrow
  Against the far, blue sky.
Has not the purple of her vesture's lining
  Brought calm and rest to all?
Has her dark robe had naught of golden shining
  Been naught but pleasure's pall?
Who knows? Perhaps when to the world returning
  In youth's light joyousness,
We'll wear some rarer jewels we found burning
  In Lent's black-bordered dress.
So hand in hand with fitful March she lingers
  To beg the crowning grace
Of lifting with her pure and holy fingers
  The veil from April's face.
Sweet, rosy April—laughing, sighing, waiting
  Until the gateway swings,
And she and Lent can kiss between the grating
  Of Easter's tissue wings.
Too brief the bliss—the parting comes with sorrow.
  Good-bye dear Lent, good-bye!
We'll watch your fading wings outlined to-morrow
  Against the far blue sky.

Erie Waters

A dash of yellow sand,
Wind-scattered and sun-tanned;
Some waves that curl and cream along the margin of the strand;
And, creeping close to these
Long shores that lounge at ease,
Old Erie rocks and ripples to a fresh sou'-western breeze.

A sky of blue and grey;
Some stormy clouds that play
At scurrying up with ragged edge, then laughing blow away,
Just leaving in their trail
Some snatches of a gale;
To whistling summer winds we lift a single daring sail.

O! wind so sweet and swift,
O! danger-freighted gift
Bestowed on Erie with her waves that foam and fall and lift,
We laugh in your wild face,
And break into a race
With flying clouds and tossing gulls that weave and interlace.

The White Wampum

The Flight of the Crows

The autumn afternoon is dying o'er
  The quiet western valley where I lie
Beneath the maples on the river shore,
  Where tinted leaves, blue waters and fair sky
  Environ all; and far above some birds are flying by

To seek their evening haven in the breast
  And calm embrace of silence, while they sing
Te Deums to the night, invoking rest
  For busy chirping voice and tired wing—
  And in the hush of sleeping trees their sleeping cradles swing.

In forest arms the night will soonest creep,
  Where sombre pines a lullaby intone,
Where Nature's children curl themselves to sleep,
  And all is still at last, save where alone
  A band of black, belated crows arrive from lands unknown.

Strange sojourn has been theirs since waking day,
  Strange sights and cities in their wanderings blend
With fields of yellow maize, and leagues away
  With rivers where their sweeping waters wend
  Past velvet banks to rocky shores, in canyons bold to end.

O'er what vast lakes that stretch superbly dead,
  Till lashed to life by storm-clouds, have they flown?
In what wild lands, in laggard flight have led
  Their aerial career unseen, unknown,
  'Till now with twilight come their cries in lonely monotone?

The flapping of their pinions in the air
  Dies in the hush of distance, while they light
Within the fir tops, weirdly black and bare,
  That stand with giant strength and peerless height,
  To shelter fairy, bird and beast throughout the closing night.

Strange black and princely pirates of the skies,
  Would that your wind-tossed travels I could know!
Would that my soul could see, and, seeing, rise
  To unrestricted life where ebb and flow

Of Nature's pulse would constitute a wider life below!

Could I but live just here in Freedom's arms,
  A kingly life without a sovereign's care!
Vain dreams! Day hides with closing wings her charms,
  And all is cradled in repose, save where
  Yon band of black, belated crows still frets the evening air.

Moonset

Idles the night wind through the dreaming firs,
That waking murmur low,
As some lost melody returning stirs
The love of long ago;
And through the far, cool distance, zephyr fanned.
The moon is sinking into shadow-land.

The troubled night-bird, calling plaintively,
Wanders on restless wing;
The cedars, chanting vespers to the sea,
Await its answering,
That comes in wash of waves along the strand,
The while the moon slips into shadow-land.

O! soft responsive voices of the night
I join your minstrelsy,
And call across the fading silver light
As something calls to me;
I may not all your meaning understand,
But I have touched your soul in shadow-land.

The White Wampum

Marshlands

A thin wet sky, that yellows at the rim,
And meets with sun-lost lip the marsh's brim.

The pools low lying, dank with moss and mould,
Glint through their mildews like large cups of gold.

Among the wild rice in the still lagoon,
In monotone the lizard shrills his tune.

The wild goose, homing, seeks a sheltering,
Where rushes grow, and oozing lichens cling.

Late cranes with heavy wing, and lazy flight,
Sail up the silence with the nearing night.

And like a spirit, swathed in some soft veil,
Steals twilight and its shadows o'er the swale.

Hushed lie the sedges, and the vapours creep,
Thick, grey and humid, while the marshes sleep.

Joe

An Etching

A meadow brown; across the yonder edge
A zigzag fence is ambling; here a wedge
Of underbush has cleft its course in twain,
Till where beyond it staggers up again;
The long, grey rails stretch in a broken line
Their ragged length of rough, split forest pine,
And in their zigzag tottering have reeled
In drunken efforts to enclose the field,
Which carries on its breast, September born,
A patch of rustling, yellow, Indian corn.
Beyond its shrivelled tassels, perched upon
The topmost rail, sits Joe, the settler's son,
A little semi-savage boy of nine.
Now dozing in the warmth of Nature's wine,
His face the sun has tampered with, and wrought,
By heated kisses, mischief, and has brought
Some vagrant freckles, while from here and there
A few wild locks of vagabond brown hair
Escape the old straw hat the sun looks through,
And blinks to meet his Irish eyes of blue.
Barefooted, innocent of coat or vest,
His grey checked shirt unbuttoned at his chest,
Both hardy hands within their usual nest—
His breeches pockets—so, he waits to rest
His little fingers, somewhat tired and worn,
That all day long were husking Indian corn.
His drowsy lids snap at some trivial sound,
With lazy yawns he slips towards the ground,
Then with an idle whistle lifts his load
And shambles home along the country road
That stretches on, fringed out with stumps and weeds,
And finally unto the backwoods leads,
Where forests wait with giant trunk and bough
The axe of pioneer, the settler's plough.

The White Wampum

Shadow River

Muskoka

A stream of tender gladness,
Of filmy sun, and opal tinted skies;
Of warm midsummer air that lightly lies
In mystic rings,
Where softly swings
The music of a thousand wings
That almost tones to sadness.

Midway 'twixt earth and heaven,
A bubble in the pearly air, I seem
To float upon the sapphire floor, a dream
Of clouds of snow,
Above, below,
Drift with my drifting, dim and slow,
As twilight drifts to even.

The little fern-leaf, bending
Upon the brink, its green reflection greets,
And kisses soft the shadow that it meets
With touch so fine,
The border line
The keenest vision can't define;
So perfect is the blending.

The far, fir trees that cover
The brownish hills with needles green and gold,
The arching elms o'erhead, vinegrown and old,
Repictured are
Beneath me far,
Where not a ripple moves to mar
Shades underneath, or over.

Mine is the undertone;
The beauty, strength, and power of the land
Will never stir or bend at my command;
But all the shade
Is marred or made,
If I but dip my paddle blade;

And it is mine alone.

O! pathless world of seeming!
O! pathless life of mine whose deep ideal
Is more my own than ever was the real.
For others Fame
And Love's red flame,
And yellow gold: I only claim
The shadows and the dreaming.

Rainfall

From out the west, where darkling storm-clouds float,
The 'waking wind pipes soft its rising note.

From out the west, o'erhung with fringes grey,
The wind preludes with sighs its roundelay,

Then blowing, singing, piping, laughing loud,
It scurries on before the grey storm-cloud;

Across the hollow and along the hill
It whips and whirls among the maples, till

With boughs upbent, and green of leaves blown wide,
The silver shines upon their underside.

A gusty freshening of humid air,
With showers laden, and with fragrance rare;

And now a little sprinkle, with a dash
Of great cool drops that fall with sudden splash;

Then over field and hollow, grass and grain,
The loud, crisp whiteness of the nearing rain.

The White Wampum

Under Canvas

In Muskoka

Lichens of green and grey on every side;
And green and grey the rocks beneath our feet;
Above our heads the canvas stretching wide;
And over all, enchantment rare and sweet.

Fair Rosseau slumbers in an atmosphere
That kisses her to passionless soft dreams.
O! joy of living we have found thee here,
And life lacks nothing, so complete it seems.

The velvet air, stirred by some elfin wings,
Comes swinging up the waters and then stills
Its voice so low that floating by it sings
Like distant harps among the distant hills.

Across the lake the rugged islands lie,
Fir-crowned and grim; and further in the view
Some shadows seeming swung 'twixt cloud and sky,
Are countless shores, a symphony of blue.

Some northern sorceress, when day is done,
Hovers where cliffs uplift their gaunt grey steeps,
Bewitching to vermilion Rosseau's sun,
That in a liquid mass of rubies sleeps.

The scent of burning leaves, the camp-fire's blaze,
The great logs cracking in the brilliant flame,
The groups grotesque, on which the firelight plays,
Are pictures which Muskoka twilights frame.

And Night, star-crested, wanders up the mere
With opiates for idleness to quaff,
And while she ministers, far off I hear
The owl's uncanny cry, the wild loon's laugh.

The Birds' Lullaby

I

Sing to us, cedars; the twilight is creeping
  With shadowy garments, the wilderness through;
All day we have carolled, and now would be sleeping,
  So echo the anthems we warbled to you;
    While we swing, swing,
    And your branches sing,
  And we drowse to your dreamy whispering.

II

Sing to us, cedars; the night-wind is sighing,
  Is wooing, is pleading, to hear you reply;
And here in your arms we are restfully lying,
  And longing to dream to your soft lullaby;
    While we swing, swing,
    And your branches sing,
  And we drowse to your dreamy whispering.

III

Sing to us, cedars; your voice is so lowly,
  Your breathing so fragrant, your branches so strong;
Our little nest-cradles are swaying so slowly,
  While zephyrs are breathing their slumberous song.
    And we swing, swing,
    While your branches sing,
  And we drowse to your dreamy whispering.

Overlooked

Sleep, with her tender balm, her touch so kind,
    Has passed me by;
Afar I see her vesture, velvet-lined,
    Float silently;
O! Sleep, my tired eyes had need of thee!
Is thy sweet kiss not meant to-night for me?

Peace, with the blessings that I longed for so,
    Has passed me by;
Where'er she folds her holy wings I know
    All tempests die;
O! Peace, my tired soul had need of thee!
Is thy sweet kiss denied alone to me?

Love, with her heated touches, passion-stirred,
    Has passed me by.
I called, "O stay thy flight," but all unheard
    My lonely cry:
O! Love, my tired heart had need of thee!
Is thy sweet kiss withheld alone from me?

Sleep, sister-twin of Peace, my waking eyes
    So weary grow!
O! Love, thou wanderer from Paradise,
    Dost thou not know
How oft my lonely heart has cried to thee?
But Thou, and Sleep, and Peace, come not to me.

Fasting

'Tis morning now, yet silently I stand,
Uplift the curtain with a weary hand,
Look out while darkness overspreads the way,
     And long for day.

Calm peace is frighted with my mood to-night,
Nor visits my dull chamber with her light,
To guide my senses into her sweet rest
     And leave me blest.

Long hours since the city rocked and sung
Itself to slumber: only the stars swung
Aloft their torches in the midnight skies
     With watchful eyes.

No sound awakes; I, even, breathe no sigh,
Nor hear a single footstep passing by;
Yet I am not alone, for now I feel
     A presence steal

Within my chamber walls; I turn to see
The sweetest guest that courts humanity;
With subtle, slow enchantment draws she near,
     And Sleep is here.

What care I for the olive branch of Peace?
Kind Sleep will bring a thrice-distilled release,
Nepenthes, that alone her mystic hand
     Can understand.

And so she bends, this welcome sorceress,
To crown my fasting with her light caress.
Ah, sure my pain will vanish at the bliss
     Of her warm kiss.

But still my duty lies in self-denial;
I must refuse sweet Sleep, although the trial
Will reawaken all my depth of pain.
     So once again

The White Wampum

I lift the curtain with a weary hand,
With more than sorrow, silently I stand,
Look out while darkness overspreads the way,
    And long for day.

"Go, Sleep," I say, "before the darkness die,
To one who needs you even more than I,
For I can bear my part alone, but he
    Has need of thee.

"His poor tired eyes in vain have sought relief,
His heart more tired still, with all its grief;
His pain is deep, while mine is vague and dim,
    Go thou to him.

"When thou hast fanned him with thy drowsy wings,
And laid thy lips upon the pulsing strings
That in his soul with fret and fever burn,
    To me return."

She goes. The air within the quiet street
Reverberates to the passing of her feet;
I watch her take her passage through the gloom
    To your dear home.

Beloved, would you knew how sweet to me
Is this denial, and how fervently
I pray that Sleep may lift you to her breast,
    And give you rest—

A privilege that she alone can claim.
Would that my heart could comfort you the same,
But in the censer Sleep is swinging high,
    All sorrows die.

She comes not back, yet all my miseries
Wane at the thought of your calm sleeping eyes—
Wane, as I hear the early matin bell
    The dawn foretell.

And so, dear heart, still silently I stand,
Uplift the curtain with a weary hand,
The long, long night has bitter been and lone,
But now 'tis gone.

Dawn lights her candles in the East once more,
And darkness flees her chariot before;
The Lenten morning breaks with holy ray,
And it is day!

The White Wampum

Christmastide

I may not go to-night to Bethlehem,
Nor follow star-directed ways, nor tread
The paths wherein the shepherds walked, that led
To Christ, and peace, and God's good will to men.

I may not hear the Herald Angel's song
Peal through the Oriental skies, nor see
The wonder of that Heavenly company
Announce the King the world had waited long.

The manger throne I may not kneel before,
Or see how man to God is reconciled,
Through pure St. Mary's purer, holier child;
The human Christ these eyes may not adore.

I may not carry frankincense and myrrh
With adoration to the Holy One;
Nor gold have I to give the Perfect Son,
To be with those wise kings a worshipper.

Not mine the joy that Heaven sent to them,
For ages since Time swung and locked his gates,
But I may kneel without—the star still waits
To guide me on to holy Bethlehem.

The White Wampum

Close by

So near at hand (our eyes o'erlooked its nearness
In search of distant things)
A dear dream lay—perchance to grow in dearness
Had we but felt its wings
Astir. The air our very breathing fanned
It was so near at hand.

Once, many days ago, we almost held it,
The love we so desired;
But our shut eyes saw not, and fate dispelled it
Before our pulses fired
To flame, and errant fortune bade us stand
Hand almost touching hand.

I sometimes think had we two been discerning,
The by-path hid away
From others' eyes had then revealed its turning
To us, nor led astray
Our footsteps, guiding us into love's land
That lay so near at hand.

So near at hand, dear heart, could we have known it!
Throughout those dreamy hours,
Had either loved, or loving had we shown it,
Response had sure been ours;
We did not know that heart could heart command,
And love so near at hand!

What then availed the red wine's subtle glisten?
We passed it blindly by,
And now what profit that we wait and listen
Each for the other's heart beat? Ah! the cry
Of love o'erlooked still lingers, you and I
Sought heaven afar, we did not understand
'Twas—once so near at hand.

The Idlers

The sun's red pulses beat,
Full prodigal of heat,
Full lavish of its lustre unrepressed;
But we have drifted far
From where his kisses are,
And in this landward-lying shade we let our paddles rest.

The river, deep and still,
The maple-mantled hill,
The little yellow beach whereon we lie,
The puffs of heated breeze,
All sweetly whisper—These
Are days that only come in a Canadian July.

So, silently we two
Lounge in our still canoe,
Nor fate, nor fortune matters to us now:
So long as we alone
May call this dream our own,
The breeze may die, the sail may droop, we care not when or how.

Against the thwart, near by,
Inactively you lie,
And all too near my arm your temple bends.
Your indolently crude,
Abandoned attitude,
Is one of ease and art, in which a perfect languor blends.

Your costume, loose and light,
Leaves unconcealed your might
Of muscle, half suspected, half defined;
And falling well aside,
Your vesture opens wide,
Above your splendid sunburnt throat that pulses unconfined.

With easy unreserve,
Across the gunwale's curve,
Your arm superb is lying, brown and bare;
Your hand just touches mine
With import firm and fine,

The White Wampum

(I kiss the very wind that blows about your tumbled hair).

Ah! Dear, I am unwise
In echoing your eyes
Whene'er they leave their far-off gaze, and turn
To melt and blur my sight;
For every other light
Is servile to your cloud-grey eyes, wherein cloud shadows burn.

But once the silence breaks,
But once your ardour wakes
To words that humanize this lotus-land;
So perfect and complete
Those burning words and sweet,
So perfect is the single kiss your lips lay on my hand.

The paddles lie disused,
The fitful breeze abused,
Has dropped to slumber, with no after-blow;
And hearts will pay the cost,
For you and I have lost
More than the homeward blowing wind that died an hour ago.

The White Wampum

At Sunset

To-night the west o'er-brims with warmest dyes;
Its chalice overflows
With pools of purple colouring the skies,
Aflood with gold and rose;
And some hot soul seems throbbing close to mine,
As sinks the sun within that world of wine.

I seem to hear a bar of music float
And swoon into the west;
My ear can scarcely catch the whispered note,
But something in my breast
Blends with that strain, till both accord in one,
As cloud and colour blend at set of sun.

And twilight comes with grey and restful eyes,
As ashes follow flame.
But O! I heard a voice from those rich skies
Call tenderly my name;
It was as if some priestly fingers stole
In benedictions o'er my lonely soul.

I know not why, but all my being longed
And leapt at that sweet call;
My heart outreached its arms, all passion thronged
And beat against Fate's wall,
Crying in utter homesickness to be
Near to a heart that loves and leans to me.

The White Wampum

Penseroso

Soulless is all humanity to me
To-night. My keenest longing is to be
Alone, alone with God's grey earth that seems
Pulse of my pulse and consort of my dreams.

To-night my soul desires no fellowship,
Or fellow-being; crave I but to slip
Thro' space on space, till flesh no more can bind,
And I may quit for aye my fellow kind.

Let me but feel athwart my cheek the lash
Of whipping wind, but hear the torrent dash
Adown the mountain steep, 'twere more my choice
Than touch of human hand, than human voice.

Let me but wander on the shore night-stilled,
Drinking its darkness till my soul is filled;
The breathing of the salt sea on my hair,
My outstretched hands but grasping empty air.

Let me but feel the pulse of Nature's soul
Athrob on mine, let seas and thunders roll
O'er night and me; sands whirl; winds, waters beat;
For God's grey earth has no cheap counterfeit.

Re-Voyage

What of the days when we two dreamed together?
  Days marvellously fair,
As lightsome as a skyward floating feather
  Sailing on summer air—
Summer, summer, that came drifting through
Fate's hand to me, to you.

What of the days, my dear? I sometimes wonder
  If you too wish this sky
Could be the blue we sailed so softly under,
  In that sun-kissed July;
Sailed in the warm and yellow afternoon,
With hearts in touch and tune.

Have you no longing to re-live the dreaming,
  Adrift in my canoe?
To watch my paddle blade all wet and gleaming
  Cleaving the waters through?
To lie wind-blown and wave-caressed, until
Your restless pulse grows still?

Do you not long to listen to the purling
  Of foam athwart the keel?
To hear the nearing rapids softly swirling
  Among their stones, to feel
The boat's unsteady tremor as it braves
The wild and snarling waves?

What need of question, what of your replying?
  Oh! well I know that you
Would toss the world away to be but lying
  Again in my canoe,
In listless indolence entranced and lost,
Wave-rocked, and passion tossed.

Ah me! my paddle failed me in the steering
  Across love's shoreless seas;
All reckless, I had ne'er a thought of fearing
  Such dreary days as these,
When through the self-same rapids we dash by,
My lone canoe and I.

Brier

Good Friday

Because, dear Christ, your tender, wounded arm
  Bends back the brier that edges life's long way,
That no hurt comes to heart, to soul no harm,
  I do not feel the thorns so much to-day.

Because I never knew your care to tire,
  Your hand to weary guiding me aright,
Because you walk before and crush the brier,
  It does not pierce my feet so much to-night.

Because so often you have hearkened to
  My selfish prayers, I ask but one thing now,
That these harsh hands of mine add not unto
  The crown of thorns upon your bleeding brow.

The White Wampum

Wave-Won

To-night I hunger so,
Beloved one, to know
If you recall and crave again the dream
That haunted our canoe,
And wove its witchcraft through
Our hearts as 'neath the northern night we sailed the northern stream.

Ah! dear, if only we
As yesternight could be
Afloat within that light and lonely shell,
To drift in silence till
Heart-hushed, and lulled and still
The moonlight through the melting air flung forth its fatal spell.

The dusky summer night,
The path of gold and white
The moon had cast across the river's breast,
The shores in shadows clad,
The far-away, half-sad
Sweet singing of the whip-poor-will, all soothed our souls to rest.

You trusted I could feel
My arm as strong as steel,
So still your upturned face, so calm your breath,
While circling eddies curled,
While laughing rapids whirled
From boulder unto boulder, till they dashed themselves to death.

Your splendid eyes aflame
Put heaven's stars to shame,
Your god-like head so near my lap was laid —
My hand is burning where
It touched your wind-blown hair,
As sweeping to the rapids verge, I changed my paddle blade.

The boat obeyed my hand,
Till wearied with its grand
Wild anger, all the river lay aswoon,
And as my paddle dipped,
Thro' pools of pearl it slipped

And swept beneath a shore of shade, beneath a velvet moon.

To-night, again dream you
Our spirit-winged canoe
Is listening to the rapids purling past?
Where, in delirium reeled
Our maddened hearts that kneeled
To idolize the perfect world, to taste of love at last.

The White Wampum

The Happy Hunting Grounds

Into the rose gold westland, its yellow prairies roll,
World of the bison's freedom, home of the Indian's soul.
Roll out, O seas! in sunlight bathed,
Your plains wind-tossed, and grass enswathed.

Farther than vision ranges, farther than eagles fly,
Stretches the land of beauty, arches the perfect sky,
Hemm'd through the purple mists afar
By peaks that gleam like star on star.

Fringing the prairie billows, fretting horizon's line,
Darkly green are slumb'ring wildernesses of pine,
Sleeping until the zephyrs throng
To kiss their silence into song.

Whispers freighted with odour swinging into the air,
Russet needles as censers swing to an altar, where
The angels' songs are less divine
Than duo sung twixt breeze and pine.

Laughing into the forest, dimples a mountain stream,
Pure as the airs above it, soft as a summer dream,
O! Lethean spring thou'rt only found
Within this ideal hunting ground.

Surely the great Hereafter cannot be more than this,
Surely we'll see that country after Time's farewell kiss.
Who would his lovely faith condole?
Who envies not the Red-skin's soul,

Sailing into the cloud land, sailing into the sun,
Into the crimson portals ajar when life is done?
O! dear dead race, my spirit too
Would fain sail westward unto you.

In the Shadows

I am sailing to the leeward,
Where the current runs to seaward
    Soft and slow,
Where the sleeping river grasses
Brush my paddle as it passes
    To and fro.

On the shore the heat is shaking
All the golden sands awaking
    In the cove;
And the quaint sand-piper, winging
O'er the shallows, ceases singing
    When I move.

On the water's idle pillow
Sleeps the overhanging willow,
    Green and cool;
Where the rushes lift their burnished
Oval heads from out the tarnished
    Emerald pool.

Where the very silence slumbers,
Water lilies grow in numbers,
    Pure and pale;
All the morning they have rested,
Amber crowned, and pearly crested,
    Fair and frail.

Here, impossible romances,
Indefinable sweet fancies,
    Cluster round;
But they do not mar the sweetness
Of this still September fleetness
    With a sound.

I can scarce discern the meeting
Of the shore and stream retreating,
    So remote;
For the laggard river, dozing,
Only wakes from its reposing
    Where I float.

Where the river mists are rising,
All the foliage baptizing
    With their spray;
There the sun gleams far and faintly,
With a shadow soft and saintly,
    In its ray.

And the perfume of some burning
Far-off brushwood, ever turning
    To exhale
All its smoky fragrance dying,
In the arms of evening lying,
    Where I sail.

My canoe is growing lazy,
In the atmosphere so hazy,
    While I dream;
Half in slumber I am guiding,
Eastward indistinctly gliding
    Down the stream.

Nocturne

Night of Mid-June, in heavy vapours dying,
Like priestly hands thy holy touch is lying
Upon the world's wide brow;
God-like and grand all nature is commanding
The "peace that passes human understanding";
I, also, feel it now.

What matters it to-night, if one life treasure
I covet, is not mine! Am I to measure
The gifts of Heaven's decree
By my desires? O! life for ever longing
For some far gift, where many gifts are thronging,
God wills, it may not be.

Am I to learn that longing, lifted higher,
Perhaps will catch the gleam of sacred fire
That shows my cross is gold?
That underneath this cross—however lowly,
A jewel rests, white, beautiful and holy,
Whose worth can not be told.

Like to a scene I watched one day in wonder:—
A city, great and powerful, lay under
A sky of grey and gold;
The sun outbreaking in his farewell hour,
Was scattering afar a yellow shower
Of light, that aureoled

With brief hot touch, so marvellous and shining,
A hundred steeples on the sky out-lining,
Like network threads of fire;
Above them all, with halo far outspreading,
I saw a golden cross in glory heading
A consecrated spire:

I only saw its gleaming form uplifting,
Against the clouds of grey to seaward drifting,
And yet I surely know
Beneath the seen, a great unseen is resting,
For while the cross that pinnacle is cresting,

An Altar lies below.

. . . . .

Night of Mid-June, so slumberous and tender,
Night of Mid-June, transcendent in thy splendour
Thy silent wings enfold
And hush my longing, as at thy desire
All colour fades from round that far-off spire,
Except its cross of gold.

The White Wampum

My English Letter

When each white moon, her lantern idly swinging,
  Comes out to join the star night-watching band,
Across the grey-green sea, a ship is bringing
  For me a letter, from the Motherland.

Naught would I care to live in quaint old Britain,
  These wilder shores are dearer far to me,
Yet when I read the words that hand has written,
  The parent sod more precious seems to be.

Within that folded note I catch the savour
  Of climes that make the Motherland so fair,
Although I never knew the blessed favour
  That surely lies in breathing English air.

Imagination's brush before me fleeing,
  Paints English pictures, though my longing eyes
Have never known the blessedness of seeing
  The blue that lines the arch of English skies.

And yet my letter brings the scenes I covet,
  Framed in the salt sea winds, aye more in dreams
I almost see the face that bent above it,
  I almost touch that hand, so near it seems.

Near, for the very grey-green sea that dashes
  'Round these Canadian coasts, rolls out once more
To Eastward, and the same Atlantic splashes
  Her wild white spray on England's distant shore.

Near, for the same young moon so idly swinging
  Her threadlike crescent bends the selfsame smile
On that old land from whence a ship is bringing
  My message from the transatlantic Isle.

Thus loves my heart that far old country better,
  Because of those dear words that always come,
With love enfolded in each English letter
  That drifts into my sun-kissed Western home.

Lightning Source UK Ltd.
Milton Keynes UK
UKOW050751181012

200729UK00001B/237/P